CW00818821

by Iain Gray

Lang**Syne**

PUBLISHING

WRITING *to* REMEMBER

LangSyne

PUBLISHING

WRITING *to* REMEMBER

79 Main Street, Newtongrange,
Midlothian EH22 4NA
Tel: 0131 344 0414   Fax: 0845 075 6085
E-mail: info@lang-syne.co.uk
www.langsyneshop.co.uk

Design by Dorothy Meikle
Printed by Printwell Ltd
© Lang Syne Publishers Ltd 2019

ISBN 978-1-85217-520-7

James

MOTTO:
I love forever.

CREST:
A swan.

NAME variations include:
Fitzjames
Geames
Jaimes
St James

Chapter one:

The origins of popular surnames

by George Forbes and Iain Gray

If you don't know where you came from, you won't know where you're going is a frequently quoted observation and one that has a particular resonance today when there has been a marked upsurge in interest in genealogy, with increasing numbers of people curious to trace their family roots.

Main sources for genealogical research include census returns and official records of births, marriages and deaths – and the key to unlocking the detail they contain is obviously a family surname, one that has been 'inherited' and passed from generation to generation.

No matter our station in life, we all have a surname – but it was not until about the middle of the fourteenth century that the practice of being identified by a particular surname became commonly established throughout the British Isles.

Previous to this, it was normal for a person to be identified through the use of only a forename.

But as population gradually increased and there were many more people with the same forename, surnames were adopted to distinguish one person, or community, from another.

Many common English surnames are patronymic in origin, meaning they stem from the forename of one's father – with 'Johnson,' for example, indicating 'son of John.'

It was the Normans, in the wake of their eleventh century conquest of Anglo-Saxon England, a pivotal moment in the nation's history, who first brought surnames into usage – although it was a gradual process.

For the Normans, these were names initially based on the title of their estates, local villages and chateaux in France to distinguish and identify these landholdings.

Such grand descriptions also helped enhance the prestige of these warlords and generally glorify their lofty positions high above the humble serfs slaving away below in the pecking order who had only single names, often with Biblical connotations as in Pierre and Jacques.

The only descriptive distinctions among the peasantry concerned their occupations, like 'Pierre the swineherd' or 'Jacques the ferryman.'

Roots of surnames that came into usage in England not only included Norman-French, but also Old French, Old Norse, Old English, Middle English, German, Latin, Greek, Hebrew and the Gaelic languages of the Celts.

The Normans themselves were originally Vikings, or 'Northmen', who raided, colonised and eventually settled down around the French coastline.

The had sailed up the Seine in their longboats in 900AD under their ferocious leader Rollo and ruled the roost in north eastern France before sailing over to conquer England in 1066 under Duke William of Normandy – better known to posterity as William the Conqueror, or King William I of England.

Granted lands in the newly-conquered England, some of their descendants later acquired territories in Wales, Scotland and Ireland – taking not only their own surnames, but also the practice of adopting a surname, with them.

But it was in England where Norman rule and custom first impacted, particularly in relation to the adoption of surnames.

This is reflected in the famous *Domesday Book*, a massive survey of much of England and Wales, ordered by William I, to determine who owned what, what it was worth and therefore how much they were liable to pay in taxes to the voracious Royal Exchequer.

Completed in 1086 and now held in the National Archives in Kew, London, 'Domesday' was an Old English word meaning 'Day of Judgement.'

This was because, in the words of one contemporary chronicler, "its decisions, like those of the Last Judgement, are unalterable."

It had been a requirement of all those English landholders – from the richest to the poorest – that they identify themselves for the purposes of the survey and for future reference by means of a surname.

This is why the *Domesday Book*, although written in Latin as was the practice for several centuries with both civic and ecclesiastical records, is an invaluable source for the early appearance of a wide range of English surnames.

Several of these names were coined in connection with occupations.

These include Baker and Smith, while Cooks, Chamberlains, Constables and Porters were to be found carrying out duties in large medieval households.

The church's influence can be found in names such as Bishop, Friar and Monk while the popular name of Bennett derives from the late fifth to mid-sixth century Saint Benedict, founder of the Benedictine order of monks.

The early medical profession is represented by Barber, while businessmen produced names that include Merchant and Sellers.

Down at the village watermill, the names that cropped up included Millar/Miller, Walker and Fuller, while other self-explanatory trades included Cooper, Tailor, Mason and Wright.

Even the scenery was utilised as in Moor, Hill, Wood and Forrest – while the hunt and the chase supplied names that include Hunter, Falconer, Fowler and Fox.

Colours are also a source of popular surnames, as in Black, Brown, Gray/Grey, Green and White, and would have denoted the colour of the clothing the person habitually wore or, apart from the obvious exception of 'Green', one's hair colouring or even complexion.

The surname Red developed into Reid, while

Blue was rare and no-one wanted to be associated with yellow.

Rather self-important individuals took surnames that include Goodman and Wiseman, while physical attributes crept into surnames such as Small and Little.

Many families proudly boast the heraldic device known as a Coat of Arms, as featured on our front cover.

The central motif of the Coat of Arms would originally have been what was borne on the shield of a warrior to distinguish himself from others on the battlefield.

Not featured on the Coat of Arms, but high-lighted on page three, is the family motto and related crest – with the latter frequently different from the central motif.

Adding further variety to the rich cultural heritage that is represented by surnames is the appearance in recent times in lists of the 100 most common names found in England of ones that include Khan, Patel and Singh – names that have proud roots in the vast sub-continent of India.

Echoes of a far distant past can still be found in our surnames and they can be borne with pride in commemoration of our forebears.

Chapter two:

Norman roots

Present on British shores since the late eleventh century, 'James' is the popular forename and surname that derives from the Latin 'Jacobus', in turn derived from the Hebrew 'Yaakou', or 'Akev', indicating 'heel.'

The Old French form of the name became 'James' and it was in the wake of the Norman Conquest of 1066 that it was first introduced to Britain.

By 1066, England had become a nation with several powerful competitors to the throne.

In what were extremely complex family, political and military machinations, the monarch was the Anglo-Saxon Harold II, who had succeeded to the throne following the death of Edward the Confessor.

But his right to the throne was contested by two powerful competitors – his brother-in-law King Harold Hardrada of Norway, in alliance with Tostig, Harold II's brother, and Duke William II of Normandy.

In what has become known as The Year of Three Battles, Hardrada invaded England and gained victory over the English king on September 20 at the battle of Fulford, in Yorkshire.

Five days later, however, Harold II decisively defeated his brother-in-law and brother at the battle of Stamford Bridge.

But Harold had little time to celebrate his victory, having to immediately march south from Yorkshire to encounter a mighty invasion force, led by Duke William of Normandy that had landed at Hastings, in East Sussex.

Harold's battle-hardened but exhausted force of Anglo-Saxon soldiers confronted the Normans on October 25 in a battle subsequently depicted on the Bayeux tapestry – a 23ft. long strip of embroidered linen thought to have been commissioned eleven years after the event by the Norman Odo of Bayeux.

It was at the top of Senlac Hill that Harold drew up a strong defensive position, building a shield wall to repel Duke William's cavalry and infantry.

The Normans suffered heavy losses, but through a combination of the deadly skill of their archers and the ferocious determination of their cavalry they eventually won the day.

Anglo-Saxon morale had collapsed on the battlefield as word spread through the ranks that

Harold had been killed – the Bayeux Tapestry depicting this as having happened when the English king was struck by an arrow to the head.

Amidst the carnage of the battlefield, it was difficult to identify Harold – the last of the Anglo-Saxon kings.

Some sources assert William ordered his body to be thrown into the sea, while others state it was secretly buried at Waltham Abbey.

What is known with certainty, however, is that William in celebration of his great victory founded Battle Abbey, near the site of the battle, ordering that the altar be sited on the spot where Harold was believed to have fallen.

William was declared King of England on December 25, and the complete subjugation of his Anglo-Saxon subjects followed.

Those Normans who had fought on his behalf were rewarded with the lands of Anglo-Saxons, many of whom sought exile abroad as mercenaries.

Within an astonishingly short space of time, Norman manners, customs and law were imposed on England – laying the basis for what subsequently became established 'English' custom and practice.

It was as reward for their services to William

that a family known as 'St James', some of whose descendants later became known as 'James', was granted lands in the English county of Surrey.

But although Surrey was the original English heartland of bearers of the name, they soon came to be found throughout the length and breadth of the British Isles – stamping a significant mark on the historical record.

Considered by some authorities to have been 'The Father of Britain's Railway System', William James was the lawyer, surveyor and land agent born in 1771 in Henley-in-Arden, Warwickshire.

It was as a land agent for families that included those of Yates, in Lancashire, the Dewes family of Wellesbourne Hall, Warwickshire and the Earl of Warwick, that as a keen geologist James suggested ways in which they could exploit the mineral resources – particularly coal – on their lands.

But such resources needed to be transported as quickly and economically as possible to customers, and it was through this that James hit upon the idea of a rail transport network.

This led, in 1803, to the creation of the Bolton and Leigh Railway while, before his death in 1837, he also proposed what would become the Liverpool and

Manchester and other series of rail networks that played a key role in Britain's Industrial Revolution.

On the high seas, Sir William James was the British naval commander who, as an employee of the East India Company, was engaged in warfare with Indian native navies.

Born in 1721 in Haverfordwest, Pembrokeshire, the son of a Welsh miller, he ran away to sea when he was aged only 11.

Later appointed commodore of the East India Company's Bombay Marine Naval Forces, in April of 1755, when commanding the ship *Protector*, he attacked and destroyed the fortress of Tulaji Angre, on the western coast of India between present-day Mumbai and Goa.

Returning to England, he was later appointed chairman of the directors of the East India Company.

Created a Fellow of the scientific think-tank known as the Royal Society for his contribution to navigation techniques, he died in 1783 – five years after having been raised to the Peerage of the United Kingdom as a baronet.

Still on the high seas, Sir William Milbourne James has two decidedly different claims to fame.

Born in 1881, he was the British naval

commander who, during the First World War, commanded the 4th Battle Squadron of the Grand Fleet, while he later served during the conflict as deputy director of naval intelligence.

Serving during the Second World War as chief of naval intelligence, he died in 1973.

In addition to his naval and naval intelligence claims to fame, he is also famed as having been the subject of the Pre-Raphaelite painter John Everett Millais's painting *Bubbles*.

Millais was James's maternal grandfather and used him as a subject for a number of his paintings – most notably *Bubbles*, painted when the future naval commander was aged five and later used as an iconic advertisement for Pears soap.

It was through this that the distinguished naval figure, much to his considerable annoyance, was dogged throughout his lifetime with the nick-name of "Bubbles."

Chapter three:

Fame and infamy

Born in 1835 in Boston, John H. James was a recipient of the Medal of Honor, America's highest award for military valour in the face of enemy action.

It was during the American Civil War of 1861 to 1865, as a gun captain aboard the USS *Richmond*, during the battle of Mobile Bay of August 1864 that he performed the actions for which he was awarded the medal.

This was when, under intense Confederate fire and with the loss of several of his crewmates, he manned his gun to great effect during a two-hour naval battle; he died in 1914.

Yet another recipient of the Medal of Honor was Willy F. James, born in 1920 in Kansas City, Missouri.

It was in April of 1945, during the Second World War and as an infantry scout attached to the 104th Infantry Division, he was instrumental in launching an attack on an enemy machine-gun nest at Lippoldsberg, Germany.

Killed in the closing moments of his successful assault, it was not until 52 years after his death that he, along with six other African-American soldiers, was belatedly awarded the Medal of Honor by U.S. President Bill Clinton.

One bearer of the name with an unusual claim to fame was the actor Meyrick Edward Clifton James, better known as M.E. Clifford James, who played a significant role in duping German intelligence during the Second World War.

Born in 1898 in Perth, Western Australia, the budding actor volunteered his services to the Entertainment National Service Association, better known by its abbreviation of ENSA, at the outbreak of war in 1939.

But as was all too common at the time, when numerous 'square pegs' were placed in 'round holes', the hapless James was assigned to the Royal Army Pay Corps, based in Leicester.

Undaunted, however, he became a member on an amateur basis with the Pay Corps Drama and Variety Group – and it was about seven weeks before the Allied invasion of Hitler's 'Fortress Europe' in June of 1944 that he was spotted, by chance, by the British intelligence agency MI5.

This came about through his role in a stage production where he played the character of Britain's famed Field Marshall Bernard Law Montgomery, more popularly known as 'Monty'.

Spotting James's uncanny resemblance to the great British commander, MI5 then arranged, through none other than the actor David Niven, then serving in the British Army's film unit, for James to be invited to London for what he was initially led to believe was a screen test for a forthcoming propaganda film.

Arriving in London for his 'screen test', James learned that the true purpose of his presence was to exploit his resemblance to Field Marshall Montgomery in what turned out be one of the greatest deception exercises of the Second World War.

Codenamed *Operation Copperhead*, the deception was highly complex, but basically involved attempting to persuade German military intelligence that an Allied invasion of Europe would not take place on the beaches of Normandy – where it ultimately did – but further south in France.

James, accordingly, after having spent some time in the company of Montgomery to closely observe his speech and mannerisms, was sent in his guise to visit locations such as Gibraltar and Algiers.

This proved particularly difficult for him because, as a heavy smoker and drinker, he had to forego these pleasures in view of the fact that the person he was impersonating was noted for his abstemious habits.

But even the British troops he met were fooled as he dropped supposedly off-the cuff 'hints' – that British intelligence knew would be picked up by agents of German intelligence – that an Allied invasion, when it came, would not be on the beaches of Normandy.

The ruse, along with others, meant that many German divisions – particularly the tank units known as Panzer divisions – were deployed away from Normandy.

James, meanwhile, as the Allied armies gained a foothold in Normandy and subsequently went on to advance throughout Nazi-occupied Europe, found himself rather ignominiously transferred back to duties with the Pay Corps.

Following the end of the war and unable to find employment in the theatrical world, he was forced to apply for a time for social benefits to support his wife and two children at their home in London.

It was not until 1954, still not having received

any official acknowledgment for his role in the important deception, that James wrote the best-selling book *I Was Monty's Double*.

This became the basis five years before his death in 1963 of the film of the same name – with James achieving his one and only big screen role, by playing himself.

Away from the high seas and the battlefields, Walter James, 4th Baron Northbourne, was not only an Olympic rower but also the pioneering agriculturist recognised as having been "The Father of Organic Agriculture."

Born in 1896, son of the 3rd Baron Northbourne, he represented Oxford University in the annual boat race against Cambridge University while he was also a member of the British 'eight' team that won the silver medal in the event at the 1920 Olympics.

But it is as an agriculturist that he is better known. From his farm in Kent, he developed in the late 1930s what has become known as 'organic farming', while in 1940 he published the landmark book on the subject, *Look to the Land*; he died in 1982.

He was the father of Christopher James, 5th Baron Northbourne, the farmer and businessman born in 1926.

At the time of writing one of the 90 hereditary peers in the House of Lords, his many positions include, since 1999, chair of the Parenting Support Forum while he is also a Fellow of the Royal Institution of Chartered Surveyors.

Across the Atlantic from British shores, William James was the founding father of a famous American dynasty of bearers of the James name.

Born in 1771 in Baileborough, in the Irish county of Cavan, he immigrated to the United States at the age of 18 and went on to amass a fortune through dealing in a number of schemes and enterprises that included money lending, real estate and also the building of the Eyrie Canal.

He died in 1832, while one of his twelve children was Henry James, better known as Henry James Sr., born in Albany, New York, in 1811.

A theologian and philosopher and an advocate of what is known as 'utopian socialism', he died in 1882.

One of his sons was the great writer Henry James, born in 1843 and whose famous works include his 1879 *Daisy Miller*, the 1881 *The Portrait of a Lady*, the 1886 *The Bostonians* and the ghost story *The Turn of the Screw*.

The brother of the philosopher and psychologist William James, born in 1842 and who died in 1910 and the diarist Alice James, born in 1848 and who died in 1892, he died in 1916.

In the world of photography, William James became a pioneering photographer of Toronto after immigrating to Canada from England in 1906, when he was aged 40.

Establishing himself as a freelance photographer, he later became president of the Canadian Photographers Association; he died in 1948, while more than 6,000 of his photographs are held in the City of Toronto Archives.

Two infamous nineteenth century bearers of the James name were the American outlaws Jesse and Frank James.

Born in 1847 in Kearney, Missouri, Jesse and his older brother Frank, born in 1843 and the sons of a Baptist minister, were engaged in guerrilla warfare on the part of the Confederacy during the American Civil War.

Turning to a life of crime at the end of the conflict, they became notorious for a series of bank, train and stagecoach robberies as members of a number of outlaw gangs.

It was a fellow gang member, Robert Ford, who shot Jesse James dead in April of 1882 in the hope of collecting a reward that had been placed on his head.

Frank James, despite later being brought to trial for his crimes, managed to secure acquittals on two separate occasions.

This was as a result of complex issues involving the competing legal jurisdictions of the states of Missouri and Minnesota – where he had perpetrated the crimes.

Portrayed by the actor Jeffrey Hunter in the 1957 film *The True Story of Jesse James*, he died in 1915, while his brother is portrayed by Colin Farrell in the 2001 *American Outlaws*.

Chapter four:

On the world stage

Best known for his roles in the popular *Carry On* series of comedy films, Solomon Joel was the South African-born but British-based actor better known as Sid James.

Born in 1913 in Johannesburg, he claimed in later life that he had worked in a series of jobs in his native South Africa that included dance tutor, boxer and diamond cutter.

But the truth was that he had trained and worked as a hairdresser before, at the age of 24, taking to the stage with the Johannesburg Repertory Players and then gaining employment with the South African Broadcasting Corporation.

Serving throughout the Second World War in an entertainment unit of the South African Army, he came to Britain a year after the conflict ended to pursue a career in acting.

Following roles in television crime dramas that included *Black Memory* and *Night Beat*, his first major film role was in the 1951 *The Lavender Hill Mob*.

But it was through co-starring in the 1950s with the comedian Tony Hancock, on the radio and television productions of *Hancock's Half Hour* that he first became a household name in Britain.

His popularity grew even further through his roles in no fewer than 19 *Carry On* comedy films, including *Carry on Doctor*, *Carry on Camping* and *Carry on Cowboy*.

Also with television credits that included the sitcom *Bless This House*, he died in 1976 after suffering a heart attack while on stage at the Sunderland Empire Theatre.

One rather spooky footnote to his death is that his ghost, complete with what had been the actor's trademark dirty laugh, is said to haunt the dressing room he had used before what proved to be his final appearance on stage.

Across the Atlantic from British shores, **Clifton James**, born in 1921 in Spokane, Washington, is the American actor best known for his role of Sheriff J.W. Pepper in the James Bond movies *Live and Let Die* and *The Man with the Golden Gun*.

Credited with the role of Mrs Hudson in the 2011 film *Sherlock Holmes: A Game of Shadows*,

Geraldine James is the English actress whose television credits include the 1984 *The Jewel in the Crown* and *Blott on the Landscape*.

Born in 1950 in Maidenhead, Berkshire, her other film credits include the 1982 *Ghandi*, the 2003 *Calendar Girls* and the 2011 *The Girl with the Dragon Tattoo*.

Best known for her role from 1969 to 1974 of Beryl Hennessey in the British television sitcom *The Liver Birds* – co-starring with Nerys Hughes – **Polly James** is the English actress born in 1941 in Blackburn, Lancashire.

Also on British television screens, **Sally James**, born in 1950 in Chiswick, London, is the former co-presenter, from 1977 to 1982, along with Chris Tarrant, of the popular Saturday morning children's show *Tiswas*; other television credits include *The Two Ronnies*, *Father Dear Father* and *The Protectors*.

Born in 1942, **Anthony James** is the American actor of both television and the big screen whose film credits include the 1967 *In the Heat of the Night*, the 1969 *Sam Whiskey* and, from 1992, *Unforgiven*.

Born in 1956 in Minneapolis, John James

Anderson is the American actor better known as **John James**.

Best known for his role of Jeff Colby in the television soap *Dynasty* and its spin-off *The Colbys*, he is also known for his role from 2003 to 2004 in the television soap *As the World Turns*.

Reaching back into Britain's ancient past – as featured on television – **Bradley James** is the actor known for his role of Arthur in the highly popular *Merlin* series.

Born in 1983 in Exeter, Devon, he also appeared with Merlin co-star Colin Morgan in the 2009 BBC Wales production *The Real Merlin and Arthur*.

Considered an icon of comedy in New Zealand, William James Te Wehi Taitoka was the entertainer better known by his stage name of **Bobby T. James**.

Born in 1948 in Waikato and host of his own television show in the 1980s, he died in 1991; New Zealand's most prestigious comedy award, the Billy T. Award, is named in his honour.

Bearers of the James name have also excelled, and continue to excel, in the highly competitive world of sport.

On the fields of European football, **David James**, born in 1970 in Welwyn Garden City, is the English goalkeeper who, in addition to playing for his national team between 1997 and 2010, has also played for clubs that include Watford, Liverpool, Aston Villa, Manchester United and Bournemouth.

From football to the rough and tumble that is the game of rugby union, **Billy James** is the Welsh former international player who represented his nation between 1983 and 1987; born in 1956 in Port Talbot, the hooker also played club rugby for Aberavon.

In baseball, **Bill James** is the American historian, writer and statistician of the game who was named by *Time* magazine in 2006 in its *Time 100* list as one of the most influential people in the world.

This is because of his highly scientific analysis of the game that can help to determine how teams win or lose. Born in 1949 in Holton, Texas, his many publications include his regularly updated *The Bill James Historical Baseball Abstract*.

From the world of sport to the world of music, Jamesetta Hawkins was the American singer of rhythm and blues, soul and rock better known by her stage name of **Etta James**.

Known as "The Matriarch of Rhythm and Blues" and also by her nickname of "Miss Peaches", the multi award-winning singer was born in Los Angeles in 1938.

An inspiration for later singers who have included Diana Ross, Paloma Faith, Amy Winehouse and Adele, she enjoyed international success with songs that include her 1955 *Roll With Me, Henry*, *Something's Got a Hold on Me* and *I'd Rather Go Blind* – for which she wrote the lyrics.

An inductee of the Rock and Roll Hall of Fame, the Blues Hall of Fame and the Grammy Hall of Fame and ranked by *Rolling Stone* magazine at number 22 on its list of the 100 greatest singers of all time, she died in 2012.

Known as "The King of the Slide Guitar", Elmore Brooks was the American musician, songwriter and band leader better known as **Elmore James**.

Born in 1918 in Holmes County, Mississippi, and a major influence on other guitarists who have included Jimi Hendrix and Eric Clapton and known for blues standards that include his 1951 *Dust My Broom*, he died in 1963.

In contemporary music, **Duncan James**,

born Duncan Matthew James Inglis in 1978 in
Salisbury, Wiltshire is the English singer, actor and
television presenter best known as a member of the
band Blue, first formed in 2000 along with Anthony
Costa, Lee Ryan and Simon Webbe.

Born in 1968 in Boscombe, Bournemouth,
Alex James is the English musician best known as
the bassist of the band Blur.

Also on British shores and in the world of
music, **Tony James**, born in 1953 in Market Drayton,
Shropshire, is the musician best known for having
been bass guitarist for the bands Generation X and
Sigue Sigue Sputnik.

From music to the equally creative world of
the written word, **P.D. James**, also honoured in the
Peerage of the United Kingdom as Baroness James of
Holland Park, is the best-selling crime writer born in
Oxford in 1920.

The daughter of a tax inspector and a former
tax office employee herself, the award-winning novelist
is best known for her series of books featuring the
detective Adam Dalgleish.

The first novel in the series, *Cover Her Face*,
was published in 1962, while she is also the author of
the *Cordellia Gray* series of mysteries; awarded her

life peerage in 1991 and a Fellow of the Royal Society of Arts, she was inducted into the International Crime Writing Hall of Fame in 2008.

Married to the screenwriter and director Niall Leonard, Erika Leonard is the best-selling author best known by her pen-name of **E.L. James**.

Born Erika Mitchell in London in 1963, she is famed for her trilogy of erotic romance novels – *Fifty Shades of Grey*, *Fifty Shades Darker* and *Fifty Shades Free*.

The daughter of a Chilean mother and a Scottish father, her many awards include the 2012 National Book Award (UK) for Book of the Year for *Fifty Shades of Grey*.

One particularly creative bearer of the proud name of James was Richard Thomson James, better known as **Richard T. James** – inventor of the popular spring toy known as the Slinky.

Born in 1914 and later graduating with a degree in mechanical engineering from Pennsylvania State University, it was during the Second World War that he hit upon the concept of what would become the Slinky.

This was when, as a naval engineer, he was tasked with devising a scheme for suspending highly sensitive shipboard instruments that would enable them to retain accuracy in high seas.

It was while utilising tension springs to aid him in his experiments that he noticed, after accidentally dropping one, that it still kept moving after it hit the ground.

This led him, in 1946, to form the James Spring Wire Company, producing the gadget known as the Slinky, and so named by his wife, Betty.

James died in 1974, while his wife died in 2008 – with millions of Slinkys having been sold since the couple first demonstrated them at the 1946 American Toy Fair.